DK READERS

3 READING ALONE

Greek Myths

Written by Deborah Lock

DK

DK Publishing

Stories of old

In ancient times, the people of Greece built huge temples where they worshipped their gods and goddesses. Where did the idea of these gods come from? Like all cultures, the Greeks wanted to understand the changing seasons, the weather, why good and bad things happened to them, and what would happen when they died.

A Note to Parents

DK READERS is a compelling program for beginning readers, designed in conjunction with leading literacy experts, including Dr. Linda Gambrell, Distinguished Professor of Education at Clemson University. Dr. Gambrell has served as president of the National Reading Conference, the College Reading Association, and the International Reading Association.

Beautiful illustrations and superb full-color photographs combine with engaging, easy-to-read stories to offer a fresh approach to each subject in the series. Each DK READER is guaranteed to capture a child's interest while developing his or her reading skills, general knowledge, and love of reading.

The five levels of DK READERS are aimed at different reading abilities, enabling you to choose the books that are exactly right for your child:

Pre-level 1: Learning to read
Level 1: Beginning to read
Level 2: Beginning to read alone
Level 3: Reading alone
Level 4: Proficient readers

The "normal" age at which a child begins to read can be anywhere from three to eight years old. Adult participation through the lower levels is very helpful for providing encouragement, discussing storylines, and sounding out unfamiliar words.

No matter which level you select, you can be sure that you are helping your child learn to read, then read to learn!

DK

LONDON, NEW YORK, MUNICH,
MELBOURNE, AND DELHI

Series Editor Deborah Lock
Art Editor Clare Shedden
U.S. Editor John Searcy
Production Editor Siu Chan
Production Erika Pepe
Picture Researcher Liz Moore
Illustrators David Burroughs
and Nilesh Mistry

Reading Consultant
Linda Gambrell, Ph.D.

First American Edition, 2008
08 09 10 11 12 10 9 8 7 6 5 4 3 2 1
Published in the United States by DK Publishing
375 Hudson Street, New York, New York 10014

Copyright © 2008 Dorling Kindersley Limited

Published in Great Britain by Dorling Kindersley Limited

DK books are available at special discounts when purchased in bulk
for sales promotions, premiums, fund-raising, or educational use.
For details, contact:
DK Publishing Special Markets
375 Hudson Street
New York, New York 10014
SpecialSales@dk.com

A catalog record for this book is available
from the Library of Congress.
ISBN: 978-0-7566-4015-6 (Paperback)
ISBN: 978-0-7566-4016-3 (Hardcover)

Color reproduction by Colourscan, Singapore
Printed and bound in China by L Rex Printing Co., Ltd.

The publisher would like to thank the following for their kind permission to
reproduce their photographs:
(Key: a-above; b-below/bottom; c-center; l-left; r-right; t-top)

Alamy Images: Mary Evans Picture Library 45tl; Print Collector 29;
Percy Ryall 8; Visual Arts Library 46-47. **The Bridgeman Art Library:** Musée
Lapidaire, Vienne, France 44; Vatican Museums and Galleries, Vatican City,
Italy 15b. **Corbis:** Araldo de Luca 18, 19, 20; Kevin Fleming 26; Adam Woolfitt
38. **DK Images:** British Museum 12t, 28, 33, 35. **Michael Holford:** 16.
Mary Evans Picture Library: Chris Coupland 34; **Nilesh Mistry:** 3, 10-11,
14, 15t, 17, 21, 22, 23, 25b, 25t, 31, 39t, 40-41, 42, 43

Jacket images: Front: Illustration by David Burroughs.
Back: **Corbis:** Gianni Dagli Orti tl; **DK Images:** British Museum tr

All other images © Dorling Kindersley
For further information see: www.dkimages.com

Discover more at
www.dk.com

Contents

The belief in the Greek gods and goddesses spread throughout the ancient Greek empire.

Their answers lay in the belief that there were gods and goddesses, who took an interest in people's everyday lives. They told stories about these immortals that we call myths. These included tales of heroes, monsters, and spirits. ❖

Family of Greek gods

Let's begin at the beginning with the god of the heavens, Uranus [YOUR-uh-nus], and the earth goddess, Gaia. Their children were the race of Titans, a group of powerful giants who roamed the heavens and earth. The youngest, Cronus, the god of Time, took control when he killed his father. Aphrodite [af-ro-DIE-tee], the goddess of love, sprang from the sea as Uranus was cut into pieces.

Aphrodite, goddess of love and beauty

*Cronus,
god of time*

Uranus, god of the heavens

Cronus had three sons: Zeus [ZOOS], Poseidon [puh-SIGH-dun], and Hades [HAY-deez]. He also had three daughters: Hestia, Demeter [de-MEE-ter], and Hera [HAIR-a]. It was these immortals and their children who appeared in many of the Greek myths.

Eros

The beautiful son of Aphrodite, Eros [AIR-oss], was the god of love. In myths, he was known for shooting his arrows at people to make them fall in love.

Zeus, god of the heavens and earth

Hera, goddess of childbirth and marriage

The peak of Mount Olympus was believed to be the home of the gods.

Zeus waged a terrifying war against his father and some of the Titans, and defeated them. He then became the god of heaven and earth and went on to father many gods, goddesses, and heroes. He lived with his wife, Hera, along with Demeter, Aphrodite, and his eight immortal children on Mount Olympus, the highest mountain in Greece.

Hestia, the goddess of the home, gave up her seat on Olympus to look after the fire within the mountain. Poseidon, the god of the sea, lived in his golden underwater palace, stirring up storms and earthquakes if he was angry.

Poseidon, god of the sea

Hades was the dark god of the Underworld—the place where people went when they died.

Hades, god of the Underworld

Demeter, the goddess of crops, had a beautiful daughter named Persephone [per-SEFF-uh-nee]. Hades kidnapped Persephone and made her his wife in the Underworld. As Demeter grieved, the earth became frozen and nothing grew. Zeus ordered Hades to free Persephone.

Hades kidnapped Persephone, taking her to the Underworld.

When she saw her daughter again, Demeter's sadness melted, winter faded, and the plants grew. However, Persephone had eaten six pomegranate seeds during her time in the Underworld, so each year she had to spend six months with Hades. For the other six months, she could be with her mother, and the seasons changed to spring and summer.

Many of Zeus's immortal children had unusual birth stories. One day Zeus had a bad headache. He asked his son Hephaestus [huh-FEST-uss] to split open his head with an axe. Out sprang Athena [a-THEE-na], dressed for battle and shouting her war cry.

Just like us, these titanic Olympians had emotions such as love, jealousy, and anger. They were fascinated by people and meddled in their lives with both heroic and fateful consequences. ❖

Athena's city

Athens, the capital of Greece, was named for Athena after she won a competition against Poseidon.

Zeus and his eight immortal children

Zeus, god of thunder and lightning

Ares, god of war

Hebe, goddess of youth

Dionysus, god of wine and feasting

Artemis, goddess of the moon and wild animals

Apollo, god of light, music, and healing

Hermes, god of trade, and protector of travelers

Athena, goddess of wisdom and war

Hephaestus, god of the blacksmith's fire

Pandora's jar

According to legend, Zeus wanted to create a race of people. He ordered Prometheus [pro-MEE-thee-us], one of the Titans, to mold men and women out of clay in the likeness of the gods. Zeus then breathed life into the people.

Prometheus lived among the people and taught them how to build homes, grow plants, and hunt animals. He begged Zeus to give them fire so they could cook and make metal tools, but Zeus refused.

"It will make them as powerful as the gods," he said.

However, Prometheus stole some fire from the rising sun. When Zeus saw the people using fire, he was very angry and severely punished Prometheus.

Eternal punishment

For disobeying Zeus, Prometheus was chained to a high rock and had his liver torn out each day by an eagle. Since he was immortal, his liver grew back every night.

Zeus also wanted to punish the people, so he asked Hephaestus to make a woman in his blacksmith's fire. The gods gave her gifts, such as beauty, love, curiosity, and deceit. They named her Pandora meaning "all-gifted."

Pandora receives the gifts of beauty from Aphrodite, music from Apollo, and deceit from Hermes.

She was sent to Prometheus's brother, Epimetheus [e-puh-MEE-thee-us]. She was also given a jar, which she was forbidden to open.

Although his brother had warned him not to accept a gift from Zeus, Epimetheus was enchanted with Pandora and married her.

Pandora could not forget about the jar. One day she peeked inside and all the evils flew out into the world—
Sickness, Sin, and Death.

As she closed the lid, Hope was the only thing left in the jar. ❖

Labors of Heracles

This is the tale of the greatest and strongest of all heroes—Heracles [HAIR-uh-kleez]. He was the son of Zeus, but his mother was a mortal woman. Hera was extremely jealous of Heracles. He grew into a determined, wise young man with superhuman strength and skill.

Zeus wanted his son to become a god when he died. Hera replied, "I will only agree to this if Heracles can perform twelve labors to be set forth by his cousin Eurystheus [you-RIS-thee-us], the king of Mycenae [my-SEE-nee]".

Super strong

As Heracles lay in his cot, Hera sent serpents to kill him. Even though he was only a baby, Heracles strangled them with his bare hands.

Eurystheus hated Heracles and hoped for his death.

"Your first task is to kill the lion, which is devouring the people of Nemea," he commanded.

Heracles was called Hercules by the Romans.

Athena guided Heracles in many of his tasks.

The Nemean lion had skin that could not be pierced by weapons. So Heracles followed the lion to its cave and wrestled with it. After strangling it to death, he returned to Eurystheus, wearing the lion's skin as armor.

Heracles successfully completed task after task. His eleventh task was to steal

some golden apples that grew on a tree in a garden that was guarded by three maidens called the Hesperides [heh-SPARE-uh-deez], along with a fierce serpent.

Heracles' tasks included killing or capturing many of the fiercest mythical animals.

After seeking advice from the gods, Heracles went first to the Hesperides' father, Atlas. He was one of the Titans defeated long ago by Zeus. Atlas's everlasting punishment was to hold up the heavens on his shoulders.

"If you ask your daughters for a couple of apples," offered Heracles, "I'll hold up the heavens for a while."

Atlas agreed but asked Heracles to kill the serpent first. Heracles did this by shooting a single arrow over the garden wall. He then took up Atlas's burden. When Atlas returned with the apples, he did not want to take the heavens back.

"I'd be delighted to continue," said Heracles, "but could you just take them for a moment so that I can make a grassy cushion for my shoulder?"

When Atlas took the heavens back, Heracles picked up the apples and walked away, and went on to complete his twelfth labor.

Zeus was pleased. When Heracles died, he joined the gods on Mount Olympus. He became the guardian of the door to the heavens. ❖

Heracles' twelfth labor was to go to the Underworld and bring back Hades' three-headed dog, Cerberus.

Theseus and the Minotaur

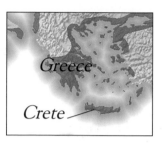

Just off the coast of Greece is an island called Crete. It was here, say the myths, that a most fearsome creature called the Minotaur lived during the reign of King Minos. The Mintoaur was half-man and half-bull and only ate human flesh. The beast was so terrible that the king commanded his greatest craftsman, Daedalus [DED-uh-lus] to build a labyrinth that no one could escape from.

Bulls of Knossos

When the ancient palace of Knossos in Crete was excavated, 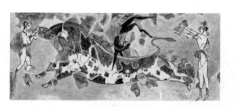 images of bulls were found. Some think this proves that the ancient Cretans worshipped bulls.

At the center of this maze lived
the Minotaur.

Every nine years, seven boys and
seven girls were sent from Athens
to be fed to the Minotaur. This was
payment from the King of Athens,
Aegeus [uh-GEE-us], for accidentally
causing the death of Minos's son many

years before. The
third payment
was now due.

In Athens, the victims were being selected. A young prince named Theseus offered to go and kill the Minotaur. He was the adopted son of Aegeus and the son of the sea-god Poseidon.

The ship that Theseus took to Crete had black sails, but this time the crew took white sails with them.

"If you succeed, raise the white sails on your return," said Aegeus to his son.

When they arrived at Crete, the Athenians were met by King Minos and his daughter, Ariadne. She fell in love with Theseus at first sight.

"I'll help you kill the Minotaur if you take me back to Athens and make me your wife," Ariadne said to Theseus. He agreed.

"Tie one end of this magical ball of thread to the entrance of the labyrinth and follow it to the center," Ariadne instructed. "Go at night while the Minotaur sleeps. After killing it, roll the thread back up and it will lead you out."

That night, the glimmering thread led Theseus to the Minotaur, which he wrestled and killed. When he arrived back at the entrance, Ariadne and the Athenians were waiting. They boarded their ship and set sail for Athens.

On the way, Theseus left Ariadne asleep on the island of Naxos because he did not love her. He also forgot to change the sails from black to white. When King Aegeus saw the black sails, he thought his son was dead and threw himself into the sea. Theseus's triumphant return was overshadowed by grief. ❖

The fall of Icarus

King Minos was furious that Theseus had succeeded in defeating the Minotaur. He put the inventor of the labyrinth, Daedalus, and his lazy son, Icarus, into prison. Daedalus started planning how to escape.

He collected feathers from passing birds and made two pairs of wings by threading the feathers together and sealing them with wax from their candles. Finally, they were ready to escape.

"Put on these wings," Daedalus told Icarus. "Follow me, and don't fly too high or too low."

They both took flight over the sea. Icarus was careful at first, but then soared upward, feeling free like a bird. The sun's heat then melted his wings and he tumbled to his death.

When Daedalus looked back for his son, he could see only feathers floating on the water. ❖

The adventures of Perseus

There was a young man named Perseus, who lived with his beautiful mother, Danae [DAN-ay-ee], on the island of Seriphos [SEH-ri-fos]. The evil king, Polydectes, wanted to marry Danae but Perseus protected her. So Polydectes tricked Perseus into attempting an impossible task.

Polydectes held a feast. Being poor, Perseus came with no gift, but he promised the king a present.

"Bring me the head of the Gorgon Medusa," challenged Polydectes.

The Gorgons were three fearsome, scaly monsters, who had snakes for hair. Anyone who looked at Medusa's face turned to stone.

Perseus's father was none other than Zeus. From Olympus, Zeus sent Athena and Hermes to help his son. They gave him the shiniest shield and the sharpest sickle in the world.

Following their advice, Perseus then visited the nymphs of the North Wind. These female spirits loaned him some winged sandals, a leather bag, and Hades' Cap of Invisibility.

Nymphs were female spirits who protected natural things such as mountains, valleys, rivers, trees, wind, and rain.

The winged horse

When Perseus killed Medusa, a winged horse, Pegasus, sprang from her body. Another myth tells how a boy named Bellerophon tamed Pegasus, using Athena's bridle.

Wearing the sandals and cap, Perseus flew unseen to the far west where he found the three Gorgons asleep. Looking only at Medusa's reflection in the shield, he cut off her head with the sickle and put it into the bag.

As Perseus flew home, he saw a beautiful princess, Andromeda [an-DRAH-muh-duh], chained to a rock. Her parents had angered Poseidon and were sacrificing her to a sea monster to appease him.

Story in the stars

Several well-known star patterns have been named after the characters in Perseus's story. These include Perseus, Andromeda, her parents, and the sea monster.

As the monster rose from the waves, Perseus held up Medusa's head and turned the monster to stone. Perseus married Andromeda and took her back to Seriphos.

King Polydectes had made Danae a slave and was surprised to see Perseus.

"Where's my gift?" he asked.

Without a word, Perseus held up the head of Medusa and turned the king to stone. ❖

The foolishness of Midas

Not all myths are about heroes.
Some tell of very foolish mortals who
misused gifts from the gods. One such
person was King Midas.

One day, Midas found an old satyr
named Silenus in his garden. Silenus
was drunk after feasting with the
god Dionysus.

Dionysus

Satyr

King Midas looked after Silenus very well and then returned him to Dionysus, who lived by the banks of the River Pactolus. In thanks, Dionysus promised Midas any gift he wanted.

"Let everything I touch turn to gold," replied Midas, greedily.

His wish was granted.

Mischievous satyrs

Satyrs were roguish male spirits of nature who roamed the woods and mountains. They were half-man and half-goat, and had horns, hooves, and tails.

With delight, Midas turned his palace and all the trees and flowers in his garden to gold.

However, his pleasure was short-lived. As he picked up food and drank his wine, they also turned to gold. Then he hugged his daughter. To his horror, she turned to gold, too.

Midas returned to Dionysus and begged to be freed from his gift.

"Wash away your greed in the spring of the River Pactolus," Dionysus told him.

As Midas bathed in the river, the water turned to gold.

However, Midas had not learned from his foolishness.

Midas was a worshipper of Pan, the mischievous goatlike god of wild places. He enjoyed listening to Pan play country tunes on his reed pipes.

One day, Pan boasted that he was a better musician than Apollo, the god of music, and challenged him to a contest.

Pan

Midas

Tmolus

Apollo

The contest was to be judged by the river god Tmolus [MO-lus]. Midas came along to listen and judge for himself.

Pan's merry tunes were no match for Apollo's lilting lyre music and Tmolus awarded the prize to Apollo. However, Midas said he preferred Pan's playing. In anger, Apollo gave Midas a pair of long, hairy donkey ears. Midas covered his ears in a turban, but people found out about them and he died of shame. ❖

Orpheus and Eurydice

The myths claim that the most gifted musician who ever lived was Orpheus [OR-fee-us]. Orpheus was married to the beautiful Eurydice [you-RIH-duh-see], but their happiness was cut short when she was bitten by a serpent and died.

Filled with aching sorrow, Orpheus took his lute and traveled to the Underworld to try and get her back. On the shore of the River Styx, he met the ferryman who rowed dead souls to the gates of Hades' kingdom. Orpheus played a sad song that charmed the ferryman into taking him across the river. At the gates, the watchdog, Cerberus, stood guard. Orpheus lulled the creature to sleep with a lullaby.

Music in his blood

Orpheus was the son of Apollo and the muse Calliope [kuh-LIE-uh-pee]. There were nine muses, or goddesses of art, who were said to inspire poets, musicians, artists, and writers.

As Orpheus made his way through the dark kingdom to see Hades, the sweet music he played soothed the screaming pain of the tormented souls.

Hades was angry that a living person had entered his realm, but when Orpheus played his music, Hades wept iron tears.

"Eurydice may follow you to the upper world," Hades said, "on the condition that you don't look at her until she has reached the sunlight." Orpheus made his way to the

surface, playing joyful tunes. But, as he reached the sunlight, he looked back.

For a moment, he saw Eurydice nearly alive again, just inside the entrance to the Underworld. Then she faded once more into a pale ghost and disappeared. Orpheus had lost her forever. ❖

Glossary

Excavate
To dig up something of historical interest.

God
A male immortal with power over nature and human affairs, who is believed in and worshipped by people.

Goddess
A female immortal with power over nature and human affairs, who is believed in and worshipped by people.

Gorgons
Three frightening female creatures with snakes for hair and golden wings.

Hero
A mortal who is known for doing great deeds.

Immortal
A supernatural being that lives forever.

Labor
A task that requires great effort.

Labyrinth
A difficult maze big enough for people to walk through.

Lute
An ancient stringed instrument similar to a guitar. It has a wooden body shaped like half a pear.

Mortal
A person who will die someday.

Mount Olympus
The highest mountain in Greece. The ancient people believed their gods and goddesses lived on the peak.

Muses
Nine sister goddesses who were said to inspire writers, poets, musicians, and artists.

Myth
A traditional story about supernatural beings and heroes.

Nymphs
Minor goddesses of nature written about in myths.

Pegasus
A winged horse that sprang from the body of Medusa.

Pomegranate
A hard, red fruit about the size of an orange, containing many large seeds within a juicy, red pulp.

Satyr
A half-human, half-animal woodland god.

Superhuman
Having greater abilities than a normal person.

Temple
A place where gods and goddesses are worshipped.

Titans
A family of giants featured in Greek myths.

Underworld
The place where ancient Greeks believed they would go when they died.

Index